RUMBLE IN THE JUNGLE
MUHAMMAD ALI·VS. GEORGE FOREMAN

BY BETSY RATHBURN
ILLUSTRATION BY EUGENE SMITH
COLOR BY GERARDO SANDOVAL

Black Sheep

BELLWETHER MEDIA • MINNEAPOLIS, MN

STRAY FROM REGULAR READS WITH BLACK SHEEP BOOKS. FEEL A RUSH WITH EVERY READ!

This edition first published in 2024 by Bellwether Media, Inc.

No part of this publication may be reproduced in whole or in part without written permission of the publisher. For information regarding permission, write to Bellwether Media, Inc., Attention: Permissions Department, 6012 Blue Circle Drive, Minnetonka, MN 55343.

Library of Congress Cataloging-in-Publication Data

Title: Rumble in the jungle : Muhammad Ali vs. George Foreman / by Betsy Rathburn ; [illustrated by Eugene Smith].
Other titles: Muhammad Ali versus George Foreman
Description: Minneapolis, MN : Bellwether Media, Inc., 2024. | Series: Black sheep. Greatest moments in sports | Includes bibliographical references and index. | Audience: Ages 7-13 years | Audience: Grades 4-6 | Summary: "Exciting illustrations follow the events of the Rumble in the Jungle. The combination of brightly colored panels and leveled text is intended for students in grades 3 through 8"– Provided by publisher.
Identifiers: LCCN 2023017821 (print) | LCCN 2023017822 (ebook) | ISBN 9798886875102 (library binding) | ISBN 9798886875607 (paperback) | ISBN 9798886876987 (ebook)
Subjects: LCSH: Boxing matches–Zaire–Kinshasa–History–20th century–Juvenile literature. | Sports rivalries–History–20th century–Juvenile literature. | Ali, Muhammad, 1942-2016–Juvenile literature. | Foreman, George, 1949–Juvenile literature.
Classification: LCC GV1127.Z35 R38 2024 (print) | LCC GV1127.Z35 (ebook) | DDC 796.83096751/12-dc23/eng/20230510
LC record available at https://lccn.loc.gov/2023017821
LC ebook record available at https://lccn.loc.gov/2023017822

Editor: Christina Leaf   Designer: Andrea Schneider

Printed in the United States of America, North Mankato, MN.

TABLE OF CONTENTS

SHAKING UP THE WORLD..............4

FACING CHALLENGES..................8

REGAINING HIS FOOTING.............14

READY TO RUMBLE!..................16

MORE ABOUT THE RUMBLE...........22
    IN THE JUNGLE

GLOSSARY...........................23

TO LEARN MORE.....................24

INDEX..............................24

Red text identifies historical quotes.

SHAKING UP THE WORLD

It is February 25, 1964. Tonight, a boxing match will decide who will be the world **heavyweight** champion. The two **contenders** gather to weigh in before the match.

Liston is the favorite to win. What is your plan for fighting him?

Float like a butterfly, sting like a bee! Hey! Rumble, young man, rumble!

Cassius Clay, Jr., a young boxer from Kentucky, will face the current champion, Sonny Liston. Clay's bold personality has drawn a lot of attention to the fight.

Liston is considered one of the best heavyweight boxers of all time. He is big and powerful. Many believe he cannot be beaten. They think Clay has no chance.

Clay does his best to distract Liston. He yells **taunts** at him that mock Liston's boxing skill.

I'm ready to rumble! I can't be beat! I'm the champ!

But Liston does not care. He believes he will knock Clay out within the first two rounds.

I want a clean **bout**. If one of you is knocked out, I'll start counting. If I count to eight, you're out. Good luck.

The two men will fight until one is knocked out. If no one is knocked out in 15 rounds, the judges will decide the winner.

When the fight starts, Clay bursts into action. He dances around the ring, dodging hits.

Liston still lands some powerful hits. His strikes to Clay's face and body come hard and fast.

In the third round, Clay gets the upper hand. He lands several powerful punches on Liston.

Liston does not give up. He attacks Clay until the end of the round, leaving Clay worn out. But despite taking some hits, Clay continues to shout taunts at Liston, trying to make him angry.

For the first time ever, Liston is cut during a fight.

ROUND
5

Before the fifth round, Clay struggles to keep his eyes open. He complains that they are burning. His trainers try to help, but it is no use.

He struggles through the round, focusing on dodging blows.

ROUND
6

Clay comes back stronger in the sixth round. But Liston seems tired. The two exchange **jabs**, but neither gains the upper hand.

ROUND
7

The seventh round starts. But Liston does not get up from his corner. Clay is awarded a **technical knockout**, or TKO.

I shook up the world!
I shook up the world!

Clay is overjoyed. The win makes him the new heavyweight champion of the world.

7

FACING CHALLENGES

Soon after becoming the heavyweight champion, Cassius Clay begins practicing **Islam**. He changes his name to Muhammad Ali to reflect his new religion. Many do not support his choices.

From Louisville, Kentucky ... the heavyweight champion of the world, Muhammad Ali!

Still, Ali is now the boxer other fighters want to beat. Other boxers line up for their chance to challenge the new heavyweight champion.

On November 22, 1965, he faces Floyd Patterson. Patterson is a two-time heavyweight champion who wants to win the title for a third time.

Throughout the match, Ali batters Patterson with punches and jabs.

By the 12th round, Patterson is looking weak. Just over two minutes into the round, the judges end the match. Ali is declared the winner by TKO.

The winner, and still heavyweight champion of the world, Muhammad Ali!

Ali's win means he keeps his title. He remains the heavyweight champion of the world.

The win against Patterson does not stop others from testing Ali. In February of 1967, Ali faces Ernie Terrell, a champion boxer who is considered Ali's most fearsome challenger.

Ready to bleed, Clay?

I'm gonna punish you!

Before the fight begins, the two trade jabs with their words. Terrell repeatedly calls Ali by his former name, Clay. This angers Ali.

During the fight, Ali is **relentless** with his punches.

It becomes clear that Terrell will lose. But Ali does not knock Terrell out. He wants to make Terrell pay for his words.

What's my name? What's my name?

The bout ends after round 15, and the judges all agree that Ali is the winner. He remains the heavyweight champion of the world. But he has lost fans. Many think he punished Terrell too harshly.

Soon after the Terrell fight, Ali faces another challenge. But this one is not in the ring.

San Francisco
Sunday Chronicle
Monday March 8th, 1965

MARINES LAND IN VIETNAM

Since 1965, the U.S. has been fighting in the **Vietnam War**. The U.S. government has carried out a **draft** that calls up American men to fight in the war.

Many Americans do not support the war. By 1967, huge anti-war protests are held in cities across the country.

In April 1967, Muhammad Ali refuses to be drafted into the U.S. Army. He is a **conscientious objector**. It is against his religion to go to war.

NO WAR

BRING OUR TROOPS HOME!!

NO WAR

No, I will not go.

Like others, he also believes the draft is unfair. Black Americans are drafted in higher numbers than white Americans. Few men from wealthy families are drafted.

Ali is stripped of his championship titles and loses his license to box because of his refusal to join. He is also charged with a crime by the U.S. government. After losing his case in court, he faces five years in prison and a $10,000 fine.

By this time, many Americans have turned away from Ali. They do not approve of his refusal to go to war. Some are upset about the beliefs he shares.

Ali does not have to stay in jail while he waits to **appeal** his case. Since he can no longer box, he starts speaking at colleges across the country to earn money.

They say I have two choices: either go to jail or go to the army.

But I would like to say that there is another alternative. And that alternative...is **justice**.

He spends the next several years sharing his beliefs on the war and the draft. He also talks about his difficulties as a Black person in the United States.

Ali's speeches, along with rising anti-war feelings across the country, help him start to regain popularity among Americans. By October 1970, his boxing license is reinstated in New York.

Ali's first big fight since 1967 is against Oscar Bonavena. Ali narrowly manages to win the tough match, but it is clear that the three years away have taken a toll. He is still a long way from regaining his championship title.

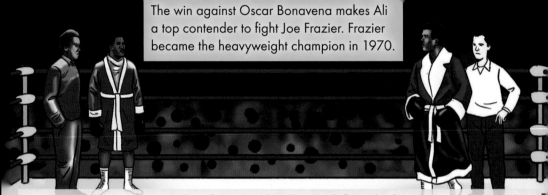

The win against Oscar Bonavena makes Ali a top contender to fight Joe Frazier. Frazier became the heavyweight champion in 1970.

Frazier has won 26 bouts without losing, making him undefeated. Ali is also undefeated. Their March 8, 1971, matchup is the first time in boxing history that two undefeated heavyweight champions will go head-to-head. They will fight 15 rounds to decide who is the top boxer.

ROUND 2

Ali takes the lead in the first two rounds. His reach is longer than Frazier's. This lets him land punches from farther away.

ROUND 4

But Frazier has a secret weapon, too. His left **hook** is one of the most powerful in boxing. He is able to repeatedly land the punch on Ali's head and body.

ROUND 6

Though both men manage to land hits, Ali is missing his usual quick, bouncing movements. He struggles to move around the ring, and Frazier backs him against the ropes again and again.

Ali is almost a sitting duck here!

Frazier is relentless. Even after several good jabs from Ali, he will not back dowr

ROUND

11

Ali manages to regain some energy and land some big hits. But by round 11, both boxers are exhausted. Neither wants to give up. A powerful left hook from Frazier sends Ali **staggering**. But he keeps fighting. The two men continue trading punches for several more rounds.

ROUND

15

Frazier starts the last round with an injury. The swelling on his face makes it so he can barely see. But early in the round, he manages to land a hit to the side of Ali's face. Ali falls to the floor.

Ali quickly gets back up and fights off Frazier until the bell ends the round, but the damage is done. In a **unanimous** decision, the judges declare Frazier the winner. It is the first loss of Ali's career.

DAILY NEWS

NEW YORK'S PICTURE NEWSPAPER

JUSTICE IS SERVED

After the loss against Frazier, Ali gets some good news. In June of 1971, after more than three years of waiting, the Supreme Court finally hears his case. They decide to clear him of all charges. He will not be punished for his refusal to join the Army.

The decision means Ali can focus on boxing full-time. He must try to work his way back up to regain the championship title.

He wins six fights in 1972.

In March of 1973, Ali faces a setback. He loses a bout with Ken Norton, leaving the fight with a broken jaw.

But six months later, Ali and Norton have a rematch. It is not Ali's strongest fight. But in the end, the judges declare him the winner.

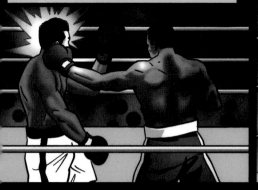

How do you feel after your win?

I'm in good condition, but I'm tireder than usual because of my age.

It is a tough win. But it gives Ali the chance to fight Joe Frazier again. Frazier is no longer the heavyweight champion, but beating him would bring Ali closer to regaining the title.

The rematch against Frazier lasts 12 rounds. Both fighters land big hits. They fight until the final bell.

The winner, by unanimous decision, is Muhammad Ali!

The judges declare Ali the winner. Now, eight years after losing his heavyweight championship title, Ali is in position to reclaim it.

To become champion again, Ali must fight George Foreman.

Foreman has recently won the heavyweight championship title from Joe Frazier in only two rounds. He has also beaten Ken Norton, the only person besides Frazier to defeat Muhammad Ali in a match.

The match will be held in Zaire, known today as the Democratic Republic of the Congo. Foreman and Ali travel there before the match to get used to the country's hot weather.

UNITED STATES

ZAIRE

Zaire has vast **rain forests**. A comment from Ali soon gives the fight its famous nickname, the Rumble in the Jungle.

I'm the real champion! There'll never be one like me!

For weeks before the fight, Ali works hard to win fans among the local people. He makes a show out of taunting Foreman, calling Foreman names and declaring himself the winner. He is confident that he will win the match.

Despite Ali's confidence, he is still considered the underdog. At 32 years old, he is [...] years older than 25-year-old Foreman. Many think he is too old to beat the champ [...]

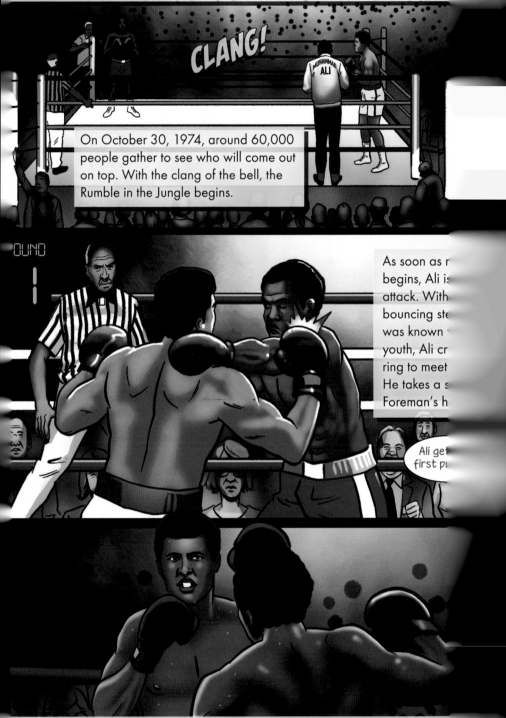

CLANG!

On October 30, 1974, around 60,000 people gather to see who will come out on top. With the clang of the bell, the Rumble in the Jungle begins.

As soon as r[...] begins, Ali i[...] attack. With[...] bouncing ste[...] was known [...] youth, Ali cr[...] ring to meet[...] He takes a s[...] Foreman's h[...]

Ali get[...] first pu[...]

oreman quickly fights back. About halfway through the first round, he backs Ali [...] p into the ropes that surround the ring. Known for his heavy punches, he swings [...] vildly at Ali's head and body. It looks to most people like an even match.

ROUND 4

By the start of round 4, Foreman's face is badly swollen.

But Ali does not soften his blows. Only seconds into the round, he deals a series of heavy hits to Foreman's head.

The three punches cause Foreman to stagger back. Ali continues his attack for the rest of the round.

Though he is on wobbly legs, Foreman stays standing for the rest of the round. As the bell clangs, he throws wild punches at Ali's head. But none land. Ali is the clear winner of round 4.

ROUND
6

Ali starts round 6 with a quick series of punches to Foreman's head.

A great left hand taken on the face of George Foreman!

In between punches, he leans back on the ropes, blocking blows from Foreman. Foreman's punches don't seem to hurt Ali. Some in the crowd wonder if leaning against the ropes is Ali's strategy to tire Foreman out.

ROUND
7

...and an **uppercut** as the round comes to a close.

Despite his earlier struggles, Foreman recovers in round 7. He manages to land a powerful left jab on Ali's face...

ROUND
8

In round 8, Foreman swings his fist toward Ali so hard that he nearly falls out of the ring.

Soon after, Ali answers with a flurry of punches that send Foreman to the floor.

4... ...5... ...6...

The crowd goes wild as Foreman lies on his back. He fails to get up in time to finish the fight.

Despite the odds, Ali has won the match.

For the second time, he is the heavyweight champion of the world. His Rumble in the Jungle with George Foreman will go down in history!

MORE ABOUT THE RUMBLE IN THE JUNGLE

- The Rumble in the Jungle fight was said to have been watched on TV by about 1 billion people around the world.

- Muhammad Ali's win marked only the second time that a boxer lost the heavyweight championship title and won it back.

- Muhammad Ali's strategy to fall back against the ropes became known as the "rope-a-dope" method. Today, it is still used to tire opponents out.

- Muhammad Ali was inducted into the International Boxing Hall of Fame in 1990. George Foreman was inducted in 2003.

RUMBLE IN THE JUNGLE TIMELINE

DECEMBER 7, 1970
Ali wins a fight against Oscar Bonavena, his first big fight after his boxing license is restored

FEBRUARY 25, 1964
Muhammad Ali beats Sonny Liston to become the world heavyweight champion for the first time

JUNE 28, 1971
The Supreme Court clears Ali of all charges

APRIL 1967
Ali is stripped of his title after refusing to serve in the Vietnam War

MARCH 8, 1971
Ali loses his first fight against Joe Frazier

OCTOBER 30, 1974
Ali regains the heavyweight champion of the world title after beating George Foreman in the Rumble in the Jungle

RUMBLE IN THE JUNGLE
KINSHASA, ZAIRE

AFRICA

GLOSSARY

appeal—to make a request to a court to reconsider a decision

bout—a fight

conscientious objector—a person who objects to something, usually military service, based on their religion or other beliefs

contenders—people who are competing against others to win

draft—a required joining of military service

heavyweight—related to the highest weight category in professional boxing

hook—a punch performed by swinging a bent arm in an arc toward an opponent

Islam—a religion that teaches belief in Allah as the only god and in Muhammad as Allah's prophet

jabs—quick punches thrown straight ahead at an opponent

justice—fair treatment

rain forests—thick, green forests that receive a lot of rain

relentless—constant, or not letting up

staggering—moving back unsteadily, as if falling

taunts—comments made to cause hurt or anger

technical knockout—the end of a fight called when judges believe a fighter can no longer continue, with the other fighter being declared the winner

unanimous—fully in agreement

uppercut—a punch delivered in an upward motion

Vietnam War—a war in Southeast Asia that took place from 1955 to 1975; U.S. troops fought in the war from 1965 to 1973.

TO LEARN MORE

AT THE LIBRARY

Buckley, James, Jr. *Muhammad Ali: The Greatest of All Time!* San Diego, Calif.: Portable Press, 2020.

Fishman, Jon M. *Boxing's G.O.A.T: Muhammad Ali, Manny Pacquiao, and More.* Minneapolis, Minn.: Lerner Publications, 2022.

O'Connor, Jim. *What Was the Vietnam War?* New York, N.Y.: Penguin Workshop, 2019.

ON THE WEB

FACTSURFER

Factsurfer.com gives you a safe, fun way to find more information.

1. Go to www.factsurfer.com
2. Enter "Rumble in the Jungle" into the search box and click 🔍.
3. Select your book cover to see a list of related content.

INDEX

Bonavena, Oscar, 11, 12
conscientious objector, 10
draft, 10, 11
Foreman, George, 16, 17, 18, 19, 20, 21
Frazier, Joe, 12, 13, 14, 15, 16
heavyweight champion, 4, 7, 8, 9, 11, 12, 14, 15, 16, 17, 21
historical quotes, 4, 7, 8, 9, 10, 11, 12, 15, 16, 17, 18, 20

Islam, 8, 10
Liston, Sonny, 4, 5, 6, 7
name, 8, 9
Norton, Ken, 15, 16
Patterson, Floyd, 8, 9
Supreme Court, 14
Terrell, Ernie, 9, 10
U.S. Army, 10, 11, 14
Vietnam War, 10, 11
Zaire, 16